Fast and Furious

Guided/Group Reading Notes
Brown Band

Contents

Introduction 2

Guided/Group reading notes

1 Character story: *The Chase*
by Anthony McGowan 12

2 Character story: *The Fun Run*
by Chris Powling 18

3 Character non-fiction: *Downhill Racers*
by Alex Lane and Tom Worsley 24

4 Variety story: *The Super Skateplank*
by Peter Corey 30

5 Variety non-fiction: *Top Speed*
by John Malam 36

OXFORD

Introduction

Reading progression in Year 3/Primary 4

By Year 3/P4, the majority of children have mastered the basics of learning to read. The focus is on continuing to build their engagement with reading, supporting reading confidence, further developing comprehension and increasing reading fluency. Phonic knowledge still plays a role in decoding some new words and in spelling but the majority of everyday words are now recognized automatically. Year 3/P4 children can read longer texts with less explicit support from repeated vocabulary and sentences and from pictures.

The texts at **brown band** contain a wide variety of sentence structures, vocabulary and verb tenses. Children will encounter complex, fast moving plots which engage interest and encourage the reader to read on through a whole book. The plot is developed over several chapters. Events are extended over a longer period of time. Some events may be told in a 'non-chronological' order through time-slip or flashback devices. Insights into characters' motives, feelings and actions become increasingly complex and characters are presented through a range of means: thoughts, feelings, behaviour, actions and responses to other characters. The consequences of actions are explored and moral dilemmas posed. Literary language is core and clearly distinct from the everyday language of character dialogue. Language play (puns, homonyms, jokes, onomatopoeia etc.) can also be found in the texts. Stories are not merely straightforward recounts but demand inference, deduction and synthesizing of information from the reader.

In non-fiction books, the content of the text is largely outside of the reader's direct everyday experience – thus broadening their knowledge and their vocabulary. Texts have depth and opportunities for the reader to infer, interpret and evaluate information – the text poses questions of the reader and encourages them to want to investigate a subject further.

The ratio of text to illustration/photographs is greater, but the illustrations continue to provide additional information and interest for the reader, including opportunities to compare and contrast visual information and source materials.

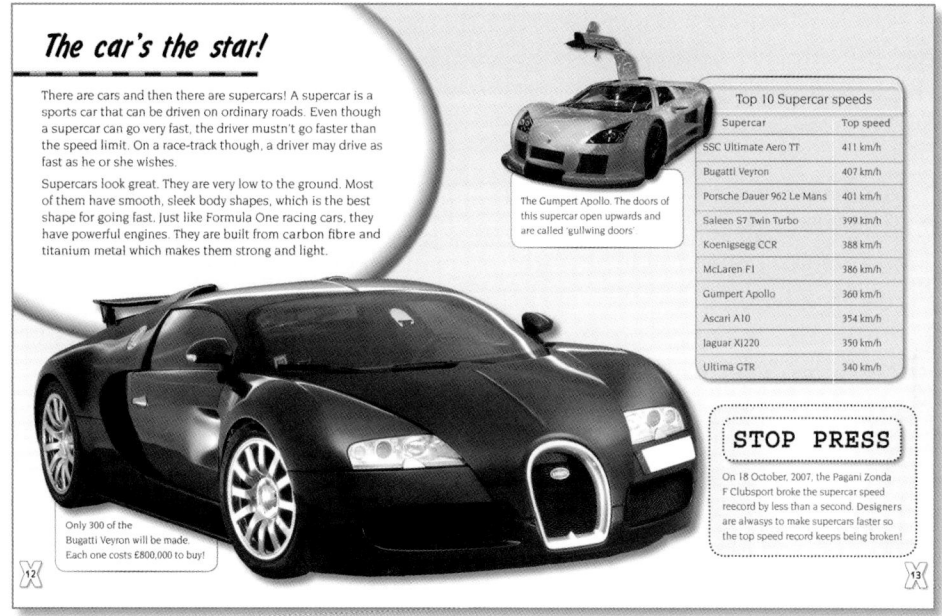

The car's the star!

There are cars and then there are supercars! A supercar is a sports car that can be driven on ordinary roads. Even though a supercar can go very fast, the driver mustn't go faster than the speed limit. On a race-track though, a driver may drive as fast as he or she wishes.

Supercars look great. They are very low to the ground. Most of them have smooth, sleek body shapes, which is the best shape for going fast. Just like Formula One racing cars, they have powerful engines. They are built from carbon fibre and titanium metal which makes them strong and light.

The Gumpert Apollo. The doors of this supercar open upwards and are called 'gullwing doors'.

Top 10 Supercar speeds	
Supercar	Top speed
SSC Ultimate Aero TT	411 km/h
Bugatti Veyron	407 km/h
Porsche Dauer 962 Le Mans	401 km/h
Saleen S7 Twin Turbo	399 km/h
Koenigsegg CCR	388 km/h
McLaren F1	386 km/h
Gumpert Apollo	360 km/h
Ascari A10	354 km/h
Jaguar XJ220	350 km/h
Ultima GTR	340 km/h

STOP PRESS

On 18 October, 2007, the Pagani Zonda F Clubsport broke the supercar speed record by less than a second. Designers are always to make supercars faster so the top speed record keeps being broken!

Only 300 of the Bugatti Veyron will be made. Each one costs £800,000 to buy!

Top Speed

A range of non-fiction features including charts, maps, tables, labelled diagrams, captions, indexes and glossaries are included to encourage children to read and interpret information presented in a variety of ways.

Familiar and regular words, now part of children's sight vocabulary, are used to provide a secure reading base. New vocabulary is increasingly varied and includes polysyllabic and more complex topic-based words. Introducing new vocabulary within a meaningful context is an important element in extending children's vocabulary range.

Visual literacy is supported through additional action and information in the illustrations, the use of graphic devices and cartoon and comic-strip genres and the suggestions for visualization comprehension strategies suggested in these notes.

Progression in the Project X character books

In this cluster, we gain new insights into the series characters – Max, Cat, Ant and Tiger – and the overall plot. In *The Fun Run*, Ant's resolve is tested when he decides to enter a charity fun run. In *The Chase*, an X-bot steals Tiger's watch and a desperate over ground and underground chase ensues to get it back.

Readers can make links to what is important in other brown band stories: *Stage Fright* (Masks and Disguises) and *Heroine in Hiding* (Heroes and Villains). Links can also be made to earlier books by, for example, tracking the evolution of the X-bots: *The Thing in the Cupboard* and *Message in an X-bot* (gold band, Communication), and *A NASTI Surprise* (lime band, Underground).

Guided/group reading

The engaging content and careful levelling of the Project X books makes them ideal for use in guided/group reading sessions. The advantages of using guided reading, as well as charts to help you assess the appropriate level for a reading group, are discussed in the *Teaching Handbook* for Year 3/P4.

To use the books in guided/group reading sessions, you should select a book at a band that creates a small degree of challenge for the reader. Typically, children should be able to read about 90% of the book unaided. This level of 'readability' provides the context for children to practise their reading and build reading confidence. The 'challenge' in the text provides opportunities for explicitly teaching reading skills.

These *Guided/Group Reading Notes* provide support for each book in the cluster, along with suggestions for follow-up activities. Books in the brown band can be covered in around three guided reading sessions. The notes for each book provide a suggested structure for several reading sessions, however, they are intended to be used flexibly.

Speaking, listening and drama

Talk is crucial to learning. Children
need plenty of opportunities to
express their ideas through talk and
drama, and to listen to and watch
the ideas of others. These processes
are important for building reading
engagement, personal response,
confidence and understanding.
Suggestions for speaking, listening
and drama are provided for
every book.

Within these *Guided/Group Reading Notes* the speaking and
listening activities are linked to the reading assessment focuses.

Building comprehension

Understanding what we have read is at the heart of reading.
To help readers become effective in comprehending a text these
Guided/Group Reading Notes contain practical strategies to
develop the following important aspects of comprehension:

- Previewing
- Predicting
- Activating and building prior
  knowledge
- Questioning
- Recall
- Visualizing and other sensory
  responses

- Deducing, inferring and
  drawing conclusions
- Determining importance
- Synthesizing
- Empathizing
- Summarizing
- Personal response, including
  adopting a critical stance.

The research basis and rationale for focusing on these aspects
comprehension is given in the *Teaching Handbook* for Year 3/P4.

Reading fluency

Reading fluency combines automatic word recognition, reading with pace, and expression. Rereading, fluency and building comprehension support each other. This is discussed more fully in the *Teaching Handbook* for Year 3/P4. Opportunities for children to read aloud are important in building fluency and reading aloud to children provides models of expressive fluent reading. Suggestions for purposeful and enjoyable oral reading and rereading/re-listening activities are given in the after reading or follow-up activities to guided/group reading and in the notes for parents on the inside cover of each book. It is worth noting that rereading activities do not have to be undertaken immediately after a book has been read.

The Project X *Interactive Stories* software can be used to provide a model of reading fluency for the whole class and/or opportunities for individuals or small groups of children to listen to stories again and again. Listening to stories being read is particularly effective with EAL children. *The Chase* from this cluster is on the *Interactive Stories* CD-ROM for Year 3–4/P4–5.

Building vocabulary

Explicit work on enriching vocabulary is important in building reading fluency and comprehension. Repeatedly encountering a word and its variants helps it become known on sight and repeated words occur throughout the books. Suggestions for vocabulary work are included in these notes. The vocabulary chart on pages 10–11 shows when vocabulary is repeated and new words introduced. It also indicates those words that can be used to support a learning alongside structured phonics and spelling programme.

Developing a thematic approach

Helping children make links in their learning supports their development as learners. All the books in this cluster focus on the theme, **Fast and Furious**. A chart showing the cross-curricular potential of this theme is given in the *Teaching Handbook* for Year 3/P4, along with a rationale for using thematic approaches. Some suggestions for cross-curricular activities are also given in these notes, in the follow-up suggestions for each book.

In guided/group reading sessions, you will also want to encourage children to make links between the books in the cluster. Grouping books in a cluster allows readers to make links between characters, events and actions across the books. This enables readers to gradually build a complex understanding of characters, to give reasons why things happen and how characters may change and develop. It helps children reflect on the skill of determining importance, as a minor incident or detail in one book may prove to have greater significance when considered across several books.

Note that the books in this cluster can be read in any order.

In the **Fast and Furious** cluster, some of the suggested links that can be explored across the books include:

- playing with toy racing cars/creating race board games **(speaking and listening, Maths)**
- exploring the impact of exercise on the human body **(Science)**
- designing a skateboard/running shoes. **(DT)**

Reading into writing

The Project X books provide both writing models and inspiration to support children's writing. Brief suggestions for relevant, contextualized and interesting writing activities are given in the follow-up activities for each book. These include both short and longer writing opportunities. The activities cover a wide range of writing contexts so writers can develop an understanding of adapting their writing for different audiences and purposes.

The Project X *Interactive Stories* software contains a collection of 'clip art' assets from the character books that children can use in their writing.

Selecting follow-up activities

These *Guided/Group Reading Notes* give many ideas for follow-up activities. Some of these can be completed within the reading session. Some are longer activities that will need to be worked on over time. You should select those activities that are most appropriate for your pupils. It is not expected that you would complete all the suggested activities.

Home/school reading

Books used in a guided/group reading session can also be used in home/school reading programmes.

Before a guided/group reading session, the child could:

- read the first chapter or section of a book
- read a related book from the cluster to build background knowledge.

Following a guided/group reading session, the child could:

- reread the book at home to build reading confidence and fluency
  - read the next chapter or section in a longer book
  - read a related book from the cluster.

Advice for parents on supporting their child with reading at home is provided in the inside covers of individual books. There is further advice for teachers concerning home/school reading partnerships in the *Teaching Handbook* for Year 3/P4.

Assessment

During guided/group reading, teachers make ongoing assessments of individuals and of the group. Reading targets are provided for each book for you to assess the children against. You should select just one or two targets at a time as the focus for the group. The same target can be appropriate for several literacy sessions or over several texts.

Readers should be encouraged to self-assess and peer-assess against the target(s).

Further support for assessing pupils' progress is provided in the *Teaching Handbook* for Year 3/P4.

 **Continuous reading objectives and ongoing assessment**

The following objectives will continue to be consolidated in guided/ group reading sessions in Year 3/P4. Teachers will be aware of these objectives in their ongoing assessment but will only specifically assess against these objectives for children who are not making the expected rate of progress:

- Read independently and with increasing fluency longer and less familiar texts **5.1**
- Know how to tackle unfamiliar words that are not completely decodable **5.3**
- Read and spell less common alternative graphemes including trigraphs **5.4**
- Read high and medium frequency words independently and automatically **5.5**

The following objective will be supported in *every* guided/group reading session and is therefore a *continuous* focus for attention and assessment (AFI). This objective is not repeated in full in each set of notes but as you listen to individual children reading you should undertake ongoing assessment against this objective as children encounter new words in their reading:

- Use syntax and context to build their store of vocabulary when reading for meaning **7.4**

Further objectives are provided as a focus within the notes for each book. Correlation to specific objectives within the Scottish, Welsh and Northern Ireland curricula is provided in the *Teaching Handbook* for Year 3/P4.

 Recording assessment

The assessment chart for the **Fast and Furious** cluster is provided in the *Teaching Handbook* for Year 3/P4.

 Diagnostic assessment

If an individual child is failing to make good progress or they seem to have a specific problem with some aspect of reading you will want to undertake a more detailed assessment. Details of how to use running records for diagnostic assessment are given in the *Teaching Handbook* for Year 3/P4.

Vocabulary chart

At Year 3/P4, children should:

- read high and medium frequency words independently and automatically
- read and spell:
  - compound words and polysyllabic words
  - prefixes and suffixes
  - unfamiliar words using known conventions.

Examples are only given in each category.

The Chase	Phonetically regular compound and polysyllabic words	swerve, slimy, gleamed, swished
	Prefixes/suffixes	-ly frantically, completely, definitely, anxiously, exactly, sarcastically, reluctantly, quickly, desperately, violently, nervously, carefully, finally
	Context vocabulary	micro-copter, pigeon, headquarters, kneepads, biscuit, teabags, sugar, bananas, shoelace
The Fun Run	Phonetically regular compound and polysyllabic words	beaming, bookmark, session, bedroom, thunderbolt, eager, progress, umbrellas
	Prefixes/suffixes	pre- precautions, prevent -able miserable, comfortable
	Context vocabulary	skateboard, micro-den, cause, weather, science, diary, ruler, internet, forecast, stomach

Downhill Racers	**Phonetically regular compound and polysyllabic words**	downhill, streamlined, skateboard, spaceman, footwear, protector, headrest, instinct, obstacle
	Prefixes/suffixes	-er -est fast, faster, fastest, great, greater, greatest, steep, steeper, steepest
	Context vocabulary	luge, speedboard, deck, trucks, axles, chassis, buttboard, aerodynamics
The Super Skateplank	**Phonetically regular compound and polysyllabic words**	board, errands, heavy, flashy, bottom, snigger, scarier, scary, technical
	Prefixes/suffixes	-ed shouted, allowed, sneered, followed, rained, dreamed, mattered, complained, scratched, added, spluttered, wondered, borrowed, realized, disqualified, launched
	Context vocabulary	Fake Ollie, helmet, pipe skaters, canal, security, officials, BMXers, handrails, helicopter, chief, judge
Top Speed	**Phonetically regular compound and polysyllabic words**	result, famous, seconds, however, replica, sleek, thrust, sprint, tilt
	Prefixes/suffixes	-er faster, quicker
	Context vocabulary	three-toed, athlete, ladies, gentlemen, surfers, carbon-fibre, titanium, supersonic, sound barrier, dragster, nitro, superfortress, hypersonic, parachute, glider, astronaut

The Chase

BY ANTHONY MCGOWAN

About this book
When a NASTI X-bot steals Tiger's watch, all of the children chase the X-bot to try and retrieve it.

You will need
- *What do you see, think, wonder?* Photocopy Master, *Teaching Handbook* for Year 3/P4
- *Vocabulary detectives* Photocopy Master, *Teaching Handbook* for Year 3/P4
- *Character logs* Photocopy Masters, *Teaching Handbook* for Year 3/P4
- *Vocabulary cards* Photocopy Master 9, *Teaching Handbook* for Year 3/P4

	Literacy Framework objective	Target and assessment focus
Speaking, listening, group interaction and drama	○ Explain, process or present information, ensuring that items are clearly sequenced, relevant details are included and accounts are ended effectively **1.2**	○ We can explain the main events of the story in a clear sequence **AF2/AF4**
Reading See also continuous reading objectives listed on page 9.	○ Use syntax, context and word structure to build their store of vocabulary as they read for meaning **7.4** ○ Explore how different texts appeal to readers using varied sentence structures and descriptive language **7.5**	○ We can collect new vocabulary from our reading **AF3/AF5** ○ We can identify effective sentences and descriptive language in our reading **AF5**

The following notes provide a structure for three guided reading sessions. They are intended to be used flexibly; you may choose to focus on all three sessions or you could focus on one session and have the children read the rest of the book independently. In Session 1, children will read to the end of Chapter 3. In Session 2 they will read Chapters 4 and 5. Children will read Chapters 6 to 9 in Session 3.

Session 1 (Chapters 1–3)

 Before reading

To activate prior knowledge and encourage prediction

- Discuss with the children what they already know about the characters in the story, and what has happened to them so far. What sort of adventures do they normally have? What does the story title suggest might happen? What sort of chase could take place? (**activating prior knowledge, predicting**)

To engage readers and support fluent reading

- Ask the children to read up to page 5. Give children the page to look at and the *What do you see, think, wonder?* Photocopy Master. Encourage children to look at the picture very carefully to make predictions about what may have happened to the watch, and what might happen next. (**predicting**)
- Read to the end of Chapter 1. Compare children's predictions with what actually happened.

During reading

- Ask the children to read Chapters 2 and 3. Listen to individual children read during this time.
- If children are using the *Character logs* Photocopy Masters encourage them to make notes. Draw the children's attention to the paragraph on page 6 when Tiger considers how each of his friends might react to the loss of the watch.

> **Assessment point**
>
> Listen to individual children reading and make ongoing assessments on their decoding, sight vocabulary, approaches to tackling new words, and their reading fluency. AF1

After reading

Returning to the text

Ask the children:

- How did the X-bot steal Tiger's watch? (**recall**)
- Where did the X-bot go? (**recall**)
- How did Cat know where the other children were? (**inferring**)

Building comprehension

- Recap with the children what happened in Chapters 2 and 3. (**summarizing**)
- Remind children of how Chapter 3 finished. Can they predict what might be in the dark corner? (**predicting**)
- The children could now draw a picture to reflect the main point of each chapter (Chapters 1–3). These pictures could be used in Session 3. (**visualizing, summarizing**)

Building vocabulary

- Draw children's attention to the author's use of language, for example, use of short sentences to build suspense (e.g. page 17), powerful verbs for speech and action (e.g. *screeched*, page 9; *roared*, page 13; *zipped*, page 14).

> **Assessment point**
>
> Can children identify the powerful verbs and discuss the impact on the reader? AF3/AF5

∙∙∙>

Session 2 (Chapters 4–5)

 Before reading

- Recap with the children what has happened in the story so far. (**summarizing, recall**)

To support decoding and word recognition and introduce new vocabulary

- In this session, children will read Chapters 4 and 5. Ask the children to flick through the chapters and note down any unfamiliar words. Encourage them to write the words on the *Vocabulary detectives* Photocopy Master. It would be helpful to enlarge this to A3 size to it can be displayed in class. Children can then be asked to try to find the meanings of the words.

- Alternatively, use the *Vocabulary cards* Photocopy Master to play snap/pairs or words-class sorting to develop familiarity with the new vocabulary. Encourage the children to find their own ways to sort and group the vocabulary e.g. words for describing speech, actions.

 During reading

- The children should independently read Chapters 4–5. As they read ask them to note down any powerful vocabulary for movement.

After reading

Returning to the text

Ask the children:

- What happened to Tiger in these chapters? (**recall**)
- Why did Max and Ant not like it in the drains? (**inferring**)

Building comprehension

- Ask children to work in a small group to imagine the scene in the sewer. They should try to imagine what the sewer would look like, how high it would be, the sounds and smells and how they might feel (**personal response, visualizing and other sensory responses**). Create an oral soundtrack of the noises that they might hear in the sewer.

- The children could now draw a picture to reflect the main point of each chapter (Chapters 4–5). These pictures could be used in Session 3. (**visualizing, summarizing**)

Building vocabulary

- This story uses powerful vocabulary for movement e.g. *whirled*; *whizzed*. Use some of these words as stimuli for movement. Encourage children to act out the vocabulary and then ask other children to suggest different vocabulary to describe the movements. You might ask children to begin to use a thesaurus to broaden their vocabulary choices.

- Discuss the author's style and use of language. Encourage children to use highlighters on copies of short sections of the story in order to pick out the different sentence types e.g. simple, compound and complex.

e.g.

Cat checked her watch. (simple sentence)
Tiger could still have gone around her, but he felt sorry for the old lady. (compound sentence)
Max tried to stay cheerful, but even he was finding it difficult as a big hairy spider crossed in front of them. (complex sentence)

· ·>

> **Assessment point**
>
> Can children identify the range of sentences and their effect? **AF5**

Session 3 (Chapters 6–9)

 Before reading

- Recap with the children what has happened in the story so far. (**summarizing, recall**) The children can then read Chapters 6 to 9 independently.

 During reading

- As you listen to individual children read, you might want to ask them to stop and summarize what has happened so far and predict what will happen next (**summarizing, predicting**).
- Alternatively, you may want the whole group to stop after page 35 and summarize what has happened so far. (**summarizing**)

 After reading

Returning to the text
Ask the children:

- What happened to each of the characters? (**recall**)

Building comprehension
- Discuss what happened in Chapters 6 to the end of the book. Draw the children's attention to the use of time slips and discuss how authors use this to maintain the pace of a story.

- The children could now draw pictures to reflect the main point of each of the chapters. (**visualizing, summarizing**)
- Ask children to use their chapter summary pictures as notes to give an oral summary of the story, thinking carefully about the sequence of events. (**summarizing**)

• >

Building fluency
- Ask children to choose one section of the story that they think has the most impact. Give them time to practise reading the section and then ask them to read it aloud to the class/group using expression.

• >

Follow-up activities

Writing activities

- Children could draw on their earlier discussions to write a short description of what it might be like to be in the sewer. (**short writing task**)
- Write a chapter story about a chase. (**longer writing task**)
- If the children have drawn a picture to reflect the main point of each chapter, they could staple them together to make a book. The children should write one or two sentences about the main point of each chapter to accompany each picture. (**short writing task**)

Cross-curricular and thematic opportunities
- Carry out races and chases with the children, and share relevant vocabulary when they have finished the exercise. (**PE**)
- Explore the impact of exercise on the human body. (**Science**)
- Think about how movement can be shown in art and cartoons. Children could make a flip book cartoon animation in which you can see movement by flicking through the pages. (**Art**)
- Make a map to show the journey that the micro-friends took in this adventure. Allow the children to experiment with their own representations of the journey. (**Geography**)

The Fun Run

BY CHRIS POWLING

About this book

In this story, Ant uses a scientific approach to help him win a fun run. On pages 41–47 there is a non-fiction section about running.

You will need

- *Email* Photocopy Master 10, *Teaching Handbook* for Year 3/P4
- *Exercise diary* Photocopy Master 11, *Teaching Handbook* for Year 3/P4

	Literacy Framework objective	Target and assessment focus
Speaking, listening, group interaction, and drama	○ Develop and use specific vocabulary in different contexts 1.4	○ We can use exciting vocabulary to record a racing commentary **AF3/5**
Reading See also continuous reading objectives listed on page 9.	○ Use syntax, context and word structure to build their store of vocabulary as they read for meaning 7.4 ○ Identify features that writers use to provoke readers' reactions 8.3	○ We can collect new vocabulary from our reading **AF2** ○ We can find ways in which a writer makes the reader react to the story **AF6**

The following notes provide a structure for three guided reading sessions. They are intended to be used flexibly; you may choose to focus on all three sessions or you could focus on one session and have the children read the rest of the book independently. In Session 1, children will read to the end of Chapter 2. Children will read Chapters 3 to 5 independently before Session 2. Session 3 focuses on pages 41–47, which the children will read during the session.

Session 1 (Chapters 1–2)

 Before reading

To activate prior knowledge and encourage prediction

● Ask the children if they know what a fun run is. Read page 3 with the group and ask them to predict what might happen in the story. (**activating prior knowledge, predicting**)

To preview the text

● Look at the picture on pages 26 and 27. What information can the children deduce about the story from the picture? (**deducing**)

To support decoding and word recognition and introduce new vocabulary

● Take a picture walk through the book and take the opportunity to introduce some of the vocabulary from the chart on page 10 of these notes. As you go through the book with the children, ask them to write down the new vocabulary.

To engage readers and support fluent reading

● Look at the title of Chapter 2: 'Under the weather'. Explain to the children that this is an idiom. To say that someone is 'under the weather' is to say that they are not feeling very well. An idiom is a word or phrase which means something different from what it says; it is usually a metaphor.

● Ask the children if they know any other idioms. Show them the following website and let them explore different idioms: www.goenglish.com/Idioms.asp

During reading

- Ask the children to read Chapters 1 and 2.
- As you listen to individual children read you might want to ask them to stop and summarize what has happened so far and predict what will happen next. (**summarizing, predicting**)
- Alternatively, you may want the whole group to stop after page 8 and recap what has happened so far. (**summarizing**)

Assessment point

Listen to individual children reading and make ongoing assessments on their decoding, sight vocabulary, approaches to tackling new words and their reading fluency. AF1

 After reading

Returning to the text
- Why did Ant say he was going to win the fun run? (**deducing**)
- How did Ant feel when he began training? (**inferring, deducing**)

Building comprehension
- Ask the children why Tiger teases Ant. (**deducing, inferring**)
- Discuss with the children how Ant feels at the beginning of Chapter 2, and how and why his feelings and attitude have changed by the end of the chapter. (**synthesizing, emphathizing**)
- Ask the children to identify any features that the author has used to provoke a reaction in the reader e.g. the use of idioms, the other characters' responses to events, similes such as 'struck him like a thunderbolt' (page 12), use of italics (page 14) and ellipsis (pages 17–19).

Building vocabulary
- Take the children on a run around the school grounds. Before setting off, talk to them about how they feel and collect the vocabulary they use. Stop them half way through the run and talk to them about how they feel now. Repeat this at the end of the run. (**sensory responses**)
- In the classroom, ask the children to think of one word that best describes how they felt before, during and after the run. (**personal response**) Now play the echo game. The children should stand in a circle. Each child takes it in turn to say their word aloud and then the rest of the class echoes it back to them. It does not matter if one child has the same word as another child. Play the echo game for 'before' the run then repeat the same activity for 'during' and 'after' the run.

Session 2 (Chapters 3–5)

 Before reading

- Recap with the children what has happened in the story so far. (**summarizing, recall**) The children can then read Chapters 3–5 independently before the session.

 During reading

- Remind children what to do if they cannot read a word, modelling with an example from the book if necessary.

 After reading

Returning to the text

- How did Ant feel at the start of the race? (**inferring, deducing**)
- How did Ant feel at the end of the race? (**inferring, deducing**)
- Why did Ant do better than the others in the race? (**drawing conclusions**)

Building comprehension

- Ask one of the children to go into role as Ant. What questions would the rest of the group like to ask him? (**questioning**)
- Remind children of the different techniques they discussed that the author used to create impact or evoke a response. Look at Chapters 3–5. What different techniques can they identify? (use of capitals, Ant talking to himself to spur himself on etc.) Discuss examples as a group.

> **Assessment point**
>
> Can children identify the different techniques that the author uses to create impact and evoke a response from the reader? **AF6**

Before reading

- Recap with the children what happened in the story. (**summarizing, recall**)
- Remind the children about Ant's scientific approach to running.

 During reading

- Ask the children to read the final section of the story (the pages from *The Science of Running*). You may want the group to note down any unfamiliar vocabulary.

· ·>

Assessment point

Can children collect new vocabulary from their reading? **AF2**

 After reading

Returning to the text

- Discuss with the group whether they do any of these things before/while they exercise, and ask them whether they have learnt anything new from this information.
- Discuss in what ways Ant followed the advice in *The Science of Running*, and how this helped him to win the race (e.g. warming up, building up slowly). (**deducing**)

Building fluency

- Ask the children to reread Chapters 3 and 4, which describe the race. Ask them to work in pairs to prepare a dramatic presentation/commentary of the race. They should narrate the action, using the text as a guide. Encourage the children to use their voices to build up tension and suspense. (**personal response**)

Follow-up activities

Writing activities

- Use the *Email* Photocopy Master to write an email to a local runner inviting them to your fun run. This activity could be extended by working in pairs and writing an email exchange, with each child adopting a character. (**longer writing task**)
- Design a poster for a fun run, encouraging all kinds of people to take part. (**short writing task**)
- Make up your own idioms. Swap ideas with a partner and see whether they can work out what the new idiom means. (**short writing task**)
- Use the *Exercise diary* Photocopy Master to keep an exercise diary. (**longer writing task**)

Cross-curricular and thematic opportunities

- Design a route for a fun run near your school. Create a map to show the route. Look at weather forecasts on the Internet or in local newspapers and consider how they might affect the run. (**Geography**)
- Collect transport to school/journey times statistics for the class. Make charts to show the information. Discuss speed aspects of car journeys to school versus health/environmental benefits of walking/cycling. Discuss safety aspects of all journey types. (**PSHE, Maths**)
- Design a miniature training course for Ant. (**DT**)
- Design shoes for Ant that could help him run in different weather conditions. (**Science, DT**)

Downhill Racers

BY ALEX LANE AND TOM WORSLEY

About this book
Downhill Racers is a non-chronological report that describes the growing sport of downhill skateboarding. It also includes biographical details of key participants presented in two ways – as fact files and as an interview.

You will need
- *Rankings* Photocopy Master 12 *Teaching Handbook* for Year 3/P4
- *Compare and contrast* Photocopy Master, *Teaching Handbook* for Year 3/P4
- *Notetaking* Photocopy Master, *Teaching Handbook* for Year 3/P4
- Large, skateboard outline shape for each child or lots of small skateboard outline shapes

	Literacy Framework objective	Target and assessment focus
Speaking, listening, group interaction and drama	○ Explain process or present information, ensuring that items are clearly sequenced, relevant details are included and accounts are ended effectively **1.2**	○ We can gather information from a text and present this to others **AF2/AF3**
Reading See also continuous reading objectives listed on page 9.	○ Identify and make notes of the main points of section(s) of text **7.1** ○ Select and use a range of technical and descriptive vocabulary **9.4**	○ We can identify the main points in a text, and make notes of these **AF2/3** ○ We can collect new vocabulary from our reading **AF2**

The following notes provide a structure for three guided reading sessions. They are intended to be used flexibly; you may choose to focus on all three sessions or you could focus on one session and have the children read the rest of the book independently. In Session 1, children will read up to page 11. Children will read pages 12 to 23 in Session 2. Session 3 focuses on pages 24 to 31.

Session 1 (pages 2–11)

 Before reading

To activate prior knowledge and encourage prediction

- Ask the children if they have heard of downhill skateboarding. If not can they infer what it might be like from the title/cover and their prior knowledge of skateboarding?

- Have children ever gone downhill on a bike/gone down a helter-skelter slide on a mat? What does that feel like/sound like? What do they see? Now consider what it must be like to go downhill on a skateboard. Collect and note some vocabulary related to speed. (**visualizing and other sensory responses**)

- Share with the children some of the challenging and technical vocabulary connected to the sport that they may be about to encounter (see vocabulary chart page 11).

To preview the text

- Look at some of the pictures and headings up to page 11. What information have they picked up from just this quick skim?

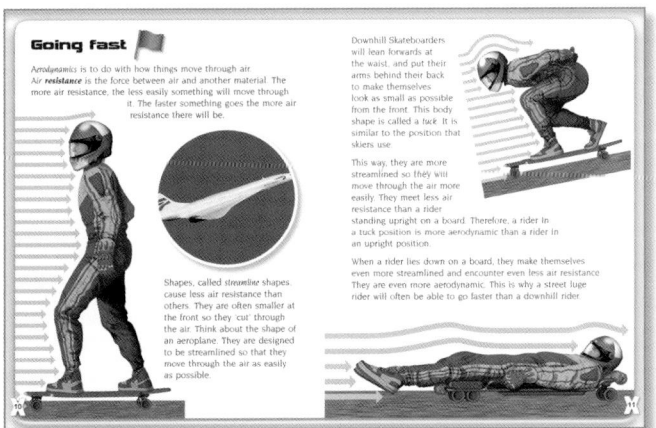

 **During reading**

To engage readers and support fluent reading

- Explain to the children that the first few pages describe what downhill skateboarding is and how it is different from ordinary skateboarding.

- Read pages 2–4 together. Model fluent reading, pausing to speculate and ask questions as you read and articulating personal responses to the text.

- Ask the children to read up to page 11 independently. You could ask them to each select a couple of spreads to concentrate on, rather than reading all the spreads.

• ➤

> **Assessment point**
>
> Listen to individual children reading and make ongoing assessments on their decoding/sight vocabulary/approaches to tackling new words and their reading fluency AF1

 After reading

Building comprehension

- Ask the children to share three facts they have learnt about downhill skateboarding with a partner. (**recall**)

• ➤

> **Assessment point**
>
> Can the children identify the main points in a text? **AF2/3**

- Ask why they think the SAFETY FIRST statement on page 7 is in capital letters. Why is it repeated? (**inferring, deducing**)

- Discuss what is meant by the sentence 'Each rider must take responsibility …' (page 6).

Session 2 (pages 12–23)

 Before reading

To support decoding and word recognition and introduce new vocabulary

- Give a large outline shape of a skateboard to each child. Scan through pages 2–11 with the children to recap some downhill racing technical terms. Check they understand this vocabulary and record it on their skateboard outlines. Explain they will be looking out for further vocabulary in this session and in Session 3.

• ➤

> **Assessment point**
>
> Can children collect new vocabulary from their reading? **AF2**

During reading

- Look at the contents page and see what topics will be covered on pages 12–23.
- Turn to pages 12–14 and challenge children to be the first to be able to tell you what a 'luge' is. Take responses and discuss.
- Ask children to read pages 12–23 independently.

 After reading

Building comprehension

- Ask the children what they think of the sport. (**personal response**)
- Ask the children how street luge and classic luge are the same and how they are different. Show the *Compare and contrast* Photocopy Master and add the headings *street luge/classic luge*. Ask them to make notes on this grid. Suggest they may want to add categories down the side of the grid such as *ride position, wheels, board design* and so on. (**recall, synthesizing**)
- Ask children to explain what makes a good racing line (racecourse) and why. (**recall, drawing conclusions**)
- Use the information on pages 20–21 to create a table showing the different types of races, how many people are involved and the outcomes. (**notetaking, summarizing**)

······································›

Building vocabulary

- Watch film clips of downhill racing. Ask children to use notebooks to record any new vocabulary they hear related to racing. Add these to their vocabulary skateboards after checking spellings in the book or in a dictionary.

> **Assessment point**
>
> Can the children identify the main points in a text, and make notes of these? AF2/3

Before reading

To engage readers

● Look at one of the rider profiles together and discuss the different information. Why do they think weight and height and date of birth are included?

● Look across all the profiles focusing on country of birth. Is this sport confined to one or two countries or is it worldwide? (**inferring, deducing**)

● Skim pages 28-31. See who it is about and the kind of questions asked. Make the point that the rider profiles and the interview are two different ways of telling us about the riders. When might they read each of these two different genres? (e.g. If they are really interested in an individual, or a sport they might want more detail than in the brief profiles. Collecting brief profiles lets you get lots of information about a range of people.)

During reading

● Remind children to be looking out for any further downhill racing vocabulary.

● Ask the children to read pages 24-31 independently.

· ·>

 After reading

Building comprehension

● Ask the children one or two recall questions from the rider profiles. (e.g. Whose nickname is Ra?) (**questioning, recall**)

● Ask the children why Tom was afraid to get back on his luge board after his accident. Why does he keep on doing it? (**questioning, inferring, deducing**)

● Ask the children to complete the *Rankings* Photocopy Master. This will encourage them to read closely and to identify detail.

> **Assessment point**
>
> Listen to individual children reading and make ongoing assessments on their decoding, sight vocabulary, approaches to tackling new words and their reading fluency. AF1

Follow-up activities

Writing activities

- Children could create 'Top Trump' style cards for a local/ favourite sports personality. (**short writing task**)
- Write and record a commentary for a downhill skateboarding race including information about the equipment, the skateboard, racing lines and any injuries during the race. (**longer writing task**)
- Ask the children to skim Tom Worsley's interview and the rest of the book for emotion words. Write an imaginary account of a race from the first person perspective, using as many of the words as you can. It could start 'After hours of patient waiting it was my turn. As I balanced on my board waiting, I felt ...'. (**longer writing task**)

Other literacy activities

- Children could use the *Notetaking* Photocopy Master grid to research the world championship. Use the book as one source and the websites given in the book as other sources. (**notetaking**)
- Suggest that children prepare and give a talk about downhill racing or create a web-page about downhill racing. (**speaking and listening**)

Cross-curricular and thematic opportunities

- Design a personalized helmet. (**DT**)
- Use the different lengths given on pages 5 and 13 to create the appropriate sized circles. (**Maths**)
- Use construction materials to create a downhill course with bends. Use different sized marbles to explore possible race lines. (**DT, Science**)
- Undertake gravity experiments as suggested on page 3. (**Science**)

The Super Skateplank

BY PETER COREY

About this book

In this story, Ben Dormer is desperate to enter a skateboarding competition, but he isn't allowed to use his home-made skateboard. He gets into trouble when he tries to buy or borrow a proper skateboard, but ends up winning the competition.

You will need
- Photocopy (ideally blown up) of three characters from the story: Ben, Cassie and Jake
- *Emotions grid* Photocopy Master 13, *Teaching Handbook* for Year 3/P4
- *Story plan* Photocopy Master 14, *Teaching Handbook* for Year 3/4

	Literacy Framework objective	Target and assessment focus
Speaking, listening, group interaction and drama	○ Develop and use specific vocabulary in different contexts **1.4**	○ We can use vocabulary to describe the different emotions and feelings of the characters **AF3/AF5**
Reading See also continuous reading objectives listed on page 9.	○ Infer characters' feelings in fiction **7.2** ○ Use syntax, context and word structure to build their store of vocabulary as they read for meaning **7.4**	○ We can infer how characters are feeling about themselves and others **AF3** ○ We can collect new vocabulary from our reading **AF2**

The following notes provide a structure for four guided reading sessions. They are intended to be used flexibly; you may choose to focus on all four sessions or you could focus on one session and have the children read the rest of the book independently. In Session 1, children will read up to Chapter 3. Children will read Chapter 4 in Session 2 and Chapters 5 and 6 in Session 3. Session 4 focuses on Chapter 7.

Session 1 (Chapters 1-3)

 Before reading

To activate prior knowledge and encourage prediction

- Ask whether any of the children in the group can use a skateboard? What can they tell the rest of the group about skateboarding? (**activating prior knowledge**)
- What do the children notice about the front cover and the title? Can they predict what the story might be about? (**predicting**)
- Read page 3 to the children. Do they know what a *Fakie Ollie* is? Why have this and other phrases such as *Dormer Stormer* been written in italics? Show the group the following website: http://www.exploratorium.edu/skateboarding/index.html and let them find out different names for skateboard moves. Can they invent some of their own names?

To preview the text

- Take a picture walk through the book and discuss what the story might be about. Focus on the expressions of the characters in the pictures and encourage children to consider what clues the expressions might give about the story. (**inferring, deducing**)

 During reading

- Ask children to read Chapters 1–3.
- Give children a copy of the *Emotions grid* on the Photocopy Master. Work together to fill in the grid up to the current chapter, tracking Ben's emotions. They can finish plotting Ben's emotions as they read through the final chapters.

Assessment point

Listen to individual children reading and make ongoing assessments on their decoding, sight vocabulary, approaches to tackling new words and their reading fluency. AF1

 31

After reading

Returning to the text

- Why could Ben not take part in the competition? (**recall**)
- What did Ben do to try and get a proper skateboard? (**recall**)
- Why did his brother not want to lend him his skateboard at first? (**deducing**)

Building comprehension

- Remind children to complete their emotions grid for this chapter.

··>

> **Assessment point**
>
> Can children make predictions about the story using evidence from the text? AF3

Session 2 (Chapter 4)

 Before reading

To support decoding and word recognition and introduce new vocabulary

- Copy and enlarge images of Ben Dormer, his brother Jake and his friend Cassie. Tell the children that you would like them to start to build a collection of words that describe the feelings of these characters at different points in the story. They can use words from the text, and also think of their own words. Display the word collection in class to support the children's reading. Use the vocabulary from the chart on page 10 to support children's understanding. Together, review Chapters 1–3 looking for suitable words to add to the collection.

> **Assessment point**
>
> Can children collect new vocabulary from their reading? AF2

··>

 During reading

- Ask children to read Chapter 4 independently. They will then discuss the chapter with a partner. As they read, ask the children to note down any more vocabulary that describes the emotions of the main characters.

After reading

Returning to the text
- Why did Ben go to the building site by the canal? (**deducing**)
- What happened when Ben entered the competition using the skateplank? (**recall**)

Building comprehension
- After reading Chapter 4, ask children to discuss it with a partner. Can they predict what might happen in the rest of the story? (**predicting**) Ask them to share their predictions with the rest of the group and compare ideas.
- Recap some of the vocabulary that has been collected to describe the emotions of the main characters. Ask children to share any new words they noted down during reading. Remind them to think not only about how the characters feel, but why they feel this way. (**inferring, empathizing**)

Session 3 (Chapters 5–6)

 Before reading

- Recap what has happened in the story so far. (**recall**)

 During reading

- Ask children to read Chapters 5 and 6 independently. Encourage them to draw conclusions about the main characters and their attitudes. (**deducing, inferring, drawing conclusions**)

After reading

Returning to the text

- Why did Ben skate off when the group of teenagers appeared? (**inferring**)
- What happened when the teenagers caught up with him? (**recall**)

Building comprehension

- Ask children to share their ideas about the emotions and attitudes of the characters with the rest of the group. (**personal response**)

Building vocabulary

- Ask children to compare and discuss their emotions grids and the vocabulary collections around the characters.

···>

Session 4 (Chapter 7)

Assessment point

Can children use appropriate vocabulary to describe the emotions of the characters? AF3

 Before reading

- Recap what has happened in the story so far. (**recall**)

 During reading

- Ask children to read the last chapter.
- Ask them to continue to track Ben's emotions on the emotions grid.

 After reading

Returning to the text

- How do the children feel about the ending? (**adopting a critical stance**)
- Who did Ben think had won the competition at first? (**recall**)

Building comprehension

- As a group, summarize the story. (**summarizing**)
- Ask children to consider the story from Brad's point of view. Ask one child to go into role as Brad and encourage the rest of the group to ask them how they feel about the competition. (**empathizing, questioning**)

- Ask children to prepare a short oral description of the main characters in the text. Remind them to use evidence from the text and make use of the vocabulary that has been collected. (**synthesizing**)

· >

Assessment point

Can children infer how characters are feeling about themselves and others? Can children use appropriate vocabulary to describe the different emotions and feelings of the characters? **AF3/AF5**

Building fluency
- After this session ask children to re-enact the chapter. Members of the group should read the story aloud using expression.

Follow-up activities

Writing activities
- The children could design a poster to announce a sporting event or competition in school. (**short writing task**)
- The children could use the *Story plan* Photocopy Master to plan and write a short story about the day they entered a competition, or the day they lost something important. (**longer writing task**)
- Write a poem about skateboarding, using the vocabulary in the story to help. (**longer writing task**)

Other literacy activities
- Carry out a talk or presentation about their favourite sport or activity. (**speaking and listening**)

Cross-curricular and thematic opportunities
- Friction: what is the effect of different surfaces on the movement of the skateboard? Set up a series of fair tests to determine the speed of different toy cars on a variety of ramps. Adjust the surfaces to provide more or less friction. Chart and compare results and draw conclusions. (**Science**)
- Design and make a streamlined skateboard. (**DT**)
- Using a digital camera, take photographs of children acting out skateboard moves. Use swirls and other digital effects to create an image of movement. (**ICT, Art**)
- Make short digital movies about a favourite sport or activity. (**ICT**)
- Organize a sports competition in school. (**PE**)

Top Speed

BY JOHN MALAM

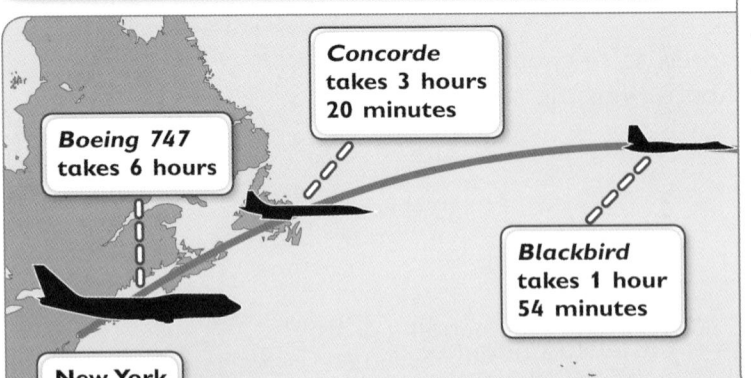

Concorde
takes 3 hours
20 minutes

Boeing 747
takes 6 hours

Blackbird
takes 1 hour
54 minutes

New York

About this book
Top Speed is a non-fiction text about everything that travels fast, from human sprinters to aeroplanes that can break the sound barrier.

You will need
- Prop box or bag with different toys linked to speed e.g. racing car, cheetah, plane, rocket, snail.
- *Speed: for and against* Photocopy Master 15, *Teaching Handbook* for Year 3/P4
- *Newspaper* Photocopy Master 16, *Teaching Handbook* for Year 3/P4

	Literacy Framework objective	Target and assessment focus
Speaking, listening, group interaction and drama	○ Sustain conversation, explain or give reasons for their views or choices **1.3**	○ We can take part in a conversation and give reasons for why we think something **AF3**
Reading See also continuous reading objectives listed on page 9.	○ Identify how different texts are organized, including reference texts, magazines and leaflets on paper and on screen **7.3** ○ Identify and make notes of the main points of sections of text **7.1**	○ We can identify different features of a non-fiction text such as tables, facts, illustrated diagrams etc **AF4** ○ We can summarize the main points of a text **AF2**

The following notes provide a structure for three guided reading sessions. They are intended to be used flexibly; you may choose to focus on all three sessions or you could focus on one session and have the children read the rest of the book independently. In Session 1, children will read up to page 7. In Session 2, children will select a two or three sections from pages 8 to 27 to present to the class. Session 3 focuses on pages 28 to 30.

Session 1 (pages 2–7)

 Before reading

To preview the text

- Look through the headings on the contents page; what do the children think they might be reading about? Are there any sections that they would particularly like to read? **(predicting, personal response)**
- Prepare a prop box or bag with different toys linked to speed. It might also provide an interesting talking point to include a slow object such as a sloth or snail. Show the objects to the children; what do they all have in common? Can they spot the odd one out?

To engage readers and support fluent reading

- Read pages 2 and 3 to the children. Would they expect a sloth or a snail to be fastest? Why do they think humans are so keen on speed? Focus on the last paragraph: *Speed can be very exciting, but in the wrong hands or on a bad day, it can be very dangerous.* What do the children think this means? Explain that you are going to discover some of the exciting elements of speed but also some of the dangers of speed. Tell them that after reading the book you would like them to write an argument about whether speed is good or not.

 During reading

- Ask the children to read pages 4–7.
- Remind the children what to do if they encounter a difficult word.

> **Assessment point**
>
> Listen to individual children reading and make ongoing assessments on their decoding, sight vocabulary, approaches to tackling new words and their reading fluency. AF1

 **After reading**

Building comprehension

● After reading pages 4–7, discuss the different ways that information has been presented in these two sections. Draw children's attention to the fact boxes, charts, labels, tables, and paragraphs of information. Discuss why the author might have chosen to present the information in different ways. Which styles do the children prefer? (**personal response**) If they had created fact boxes for the *Racing with nature* section, what might they have put in them?

● ●>

> **Assessment point**
>
> Can children use appropriate terms to describe the different presentational features? Can they explain why each might have been used? AF4

Building vocabulary

● If you have already undertaken the *Max meets Lewis Hamilton* activities, ask children to write three new words onto the racing cars and add them to the class vocabulary racing track (instructions on page 27).

Session 2 (2–3 sections from pages 8–27)

 Before reading

● Remind children that at the end of this book they will be writing a short argument for or against the use of speed. Ask them to choose two or three sections to read (from page 8, to page 26). Explain that they should become 'experts' on their chosen sections as they will be asked to summarize the information for the group.

 During reading

● As they read their chosen sections, ask them to consider points for or against speed. You might ask them to note down any particular vocabulary they want to include.

 After reading

Building comprehension

● When they have finished reading their sections, ask the children to summarize the information for the rest of the group. Ask each child to record the key points for or against speed in the Photocopy Master *Speed: For and Against.* (**summarizing, determining importance**).

• ➤

Building vocabulary

◉ Ask children to write three new words onto the racing cars and add them to the class vocabulary racing track.

Session 3 (pages 28–30)

 Before reading

◉ Discuss with the children how they feel about speed at this point, and why. (**personal response**)

 During reading

◉ Ask the children to read the final two sections (pages 28–30). As they read, ask them to continue considering points for and against speed.

 After reading

Building comprehension

◉ After reading, ask the children if their feelings about speed have changed. How do they feel about speed now? Do they know of any other problems with speed? (**Adopting a critical stance**) During the group discussion, encourage the children to give reasons to support their opinions. They should use information from the text to back up their arguments, where appropriate.

• ➤

◉ Ask them to complete their 'for and against' charts for the final sections of the book.

Building fluency

- Ask children to choose their favourite section to prepare and read to the rest of the class. Tell them that they need to read as if they are experts in the field and therefore should read with authority and appropriate expression.

Building vocabulary

- Ask children to write three new words onto the racing cars and add them to the class vocabulary racing track.

Follow-up activities

Writing activities

- Write or present a persuasive argument for or against speed. (**longer writing task**)
- Use the *Newspaper* Photocopy Master to write a newspaper article reporting a 'speed event'. (**longer writing task**)
- Create a fact-file for a person involved in a speed sport. Use information books and the internet to research the chosen person. (**longer writing task**)

Other literacy activities

- Hold a class debate: is speed a good or bad thing? (**speaking and listening**)

Cross curricular and thematic opportunities

- Ask children to run 100m, measure their speed and then work out how fast they could run 1km. Make a table and chart the speed of the different children in their class. Who can run the fastest? Ask the children to rank them in order. (**Maths/PE**)
- Explore local/national rail, road and air routes and consider why routes are where they are e.g. flat terrain, converging on city centre. Create maps showing local transport routes including bus routes, cycle paths and footpaths. (**Geography**)